SURVIVING BLACK HAWK DOWN: THE TRUE STORY BEHIND THE BATTLE OF MOGADISHU

Shocking Revelations from Soldiers and Civilians Who Survived

Susan K. Winters

Copyright © 2025 Susan K. Winters

All rights reserved

No part of this book may be reproduced, or stored in a retrieval system, or transmitted in any form or by any means, electronic, mechanical, photocopying, recording, or otherwise, without express written permission of the publisher.

Disclamier: This book serves as a movie guide and is not associated with or endorsed by the original book available on Amazon. The content provided in this guide solely intended for the purpose of enhancing the reader's understanding and enjoyment of the corresponding movie.

CONTENTS

Title Page
Copyright
Introduction   1
Chapter 1: Setting the Stage   5
Chapter 2: The Military Operation   13
Chapter 3: Chaos Unleashed   21
Chapter 4: A Day of Survival   29
Chapter 5: The Aftermath   37
Chapter 6: Untold Stories   46
Chapter 7: Lessons Learned   53
Conclusion   62

INTRODUCTION

The Battle of Mogadishu, which unfolded on October 3, 1993, is etched into the history of modern warfare as a brutal and defining moment. The conflict, which saw U.S. forces sent to Somalia in an attempt to restore order amidst a humanitarian crisis, quickly spiraled into a nightmare that would claim the lives of both soldiers and civilians alike. While the event itself was widely covered by the media, the true stories of the men who fought on the ground and the Somali civilians caught in the crossfire have often remained untold. This book aims to shed light on those stories, providing a raw, unflinching look at the horrors of war and the resilience of the human spirit.

In many ways, the 2001 film *Black Hawk Down*, directed by Ridley Scott, brought this battle to global attention. The film, based on the 1999 book by Mark Bowden, was a gripping portrayal of the chaos that ensued when two Black Hawk helicopters were shot down during a mission to capture a Somali warlord's lieutenants. The movie, which featured a star-studded cast including Josh Hartnett and Ewan McGregor, focused on the American soldiers' bravery and struggles, winning two Academy Awards and earning critical acclaim. However, *Black Hawk Down* only captured a fraction of the story. While it showcased the courage and sacrifice of U.S. forces, it largely left out the experiences of the Somali people, the true nature of the conflict, and the full scale of the consequences that followed.

This book seeks to bridge that gap by offering a more comprehensive account of the events. It will not only explore the tactical decisions and military operations that shaped the outcome of the battle but also delve deeply into the human side of the story—the fears, the losses, and the resilience of those who survived. Through a combination of firsthand accounts from soldiers who fought in the battle and civilians who lived through it, we'll uncover the untold stories that paint a fuller picture of what transpired that fateful day.

The personal experiences of the soldiers, many of whom were thrust into a situation far more dangerous than they could have imagined, are intertwined with those of the Somali civilians who had no choice but to endure the violence that ravaged their city. Their stories are often overlooked in traditional narratives of war, but they offer an invaluable insight into the true cost of conflict. By highlighting these voices, this book not only preserves the memories of those who lived through it but also provides a deeper understanding of the complex human toll that accompanies military interventions. The survivors, both American and Somali, have lived with the scars of that day for decades. Their stories, whether of courage, survival, or grief, deserve to be heard.

Ultimately, the purpose of this book is to remind readers of the immense human cost of war and the importance of seeing beyond the headlines and the Hollywood portrayals. It is not enough to simply recount the military strategy or the high-stakes operations that took place; we must also listen to the voices of those who lived it—the ones who were there, who fought, and who bore witness to the profound impact of a battle that would leave a lasting imprint on both nations. By providing these untold stories, this book seeks to honor the memories of the fallen and give a voice to those whose experiences are often forgotten in the broader narrative of war.

CHAPTER 1: SETTING THE STAGE

The Origins of the Battle

The Political Landscape of Somalia in the 1990s

The roots of the **Battle of Mogadishu** in 1993 are deeply tied to the **political chaos** and **social unrest** that plagued **Somalia** for decades prior. To understand the profound impact of the battle, it's essential to look back at the history of the nation, the tumultuous political climate, and the conditions that led to international intervention.

In the early 1980s, Somalia was governed by the regime of **Siad Barre**, a leader whose control over the country had grown increasingly **authoritarian**. Initially supported by both the **Soviet Union** and the **United States** during the Cold War, Barre's government started to lose favor in the mid-1980s as his oppressive rule and disregard for human rights became more apparent.

The country was already deeply fractured along clan lines, and Barre's harsh military tactics, aimed at consolidating power, intensified the divisions.

By the late 1980s, opposition to Barre's regime had grown significantly. A range of rebel groups, many of which were **ethnically or tribally based**, began to form in response to the government's harsh policies. **Political unrest** swept across the country, and in **1991**, the pressure from these groups finally led to the fall of Barre's government. However, the collapse of the central government didn't bring peace; instead, it resulted in a **power vacuum** that was exploited by competing **warlords**.

The civil war that followed left **Somalia in ruins**, with no clear governing body able to establish order. Local leaders, driven by personal ambition, divided the country into **territorial factions**, often using **militias** to fight over resources and influence. This fragmentation turned the country into an **anarchical state**, where the people were caught in the middle of a brutal conflict with little hope for a resolution.

At the heart of this chaos was the compounded tragedy of **famine**. As fighting between warlords intensified, agricultural systems broke down, food became scarce, and **starvation** began to spread throughout the population. The United Nations, alongside various international aid agencies, sought to provide humanitarian relief to Somalia's people. However, the ongoing violence made aid deliveries incredibly difficult, if not impossible in some regions. As millions of people were left to fend for themselves in the midst of conflict, the **Somali famine** of 1992 became one of the **worst humanitarian crises** in modern history.

In response to the dire situation, the United Nations authorized a mission called **Operation Restore Hope**, aimed at delivering food aid and establishing a semblance of order in the war-torn country. Initially, **UN peacekeepers** entered Somalia with the primary goal of securing the delivery of food and medical supplies. However, the peacekeepers quickly found themselves drawn into the conflict between the various factions. The violence was relentless, and even the most well-intentioned peacekeeping efforts were constantly undermined by the brutality of the ongoing civil war.

The situation became even more complicated as the **U.S. military** entered the scene in 1992. The United States, eager to help stabilize the situation and provide relief, joined the mission under the auspices of the **United Nations**. But the involvement of U.S. forces soon escalated beyond humanitarian aid. The peacekeeping mission took a **military turn**, and as a result, the international community found itself increasingly entrenched in a civil war with no clear path to victory or resolution.

The Rise of Warlord Mohamed Farrah Aidid

Amidst the chaos and destruction of Somalia in the early 1990s, **Mohamed Farrah Aidid** emerged as one of the most powerful and notorious figures in the country. His rise to prominence was marked by a combination of military skill, strategic alliances, and ruthless tactics.

Aidid's **influence** grew from his position as the leader of the **Habr Gidr clan**, one of the most powerful Somali clans in the country. As the central government fell and various warlords took control of different regions, Aidid established himself as a major player in the power struggle. He sought to claim control over the capital city of **Mogadishu** and its vital resources. His strategy was built on the manipulation of clan loyalties and the formation of a formidable **militia**, which he used to assert dominance.

Aidid's **power struggle** was not just political—it was also deeply **personal**. He had a longstanding feud with the leader of the **United Somali Congress** (USC), **Ali Mahdi Mohamed**, a rival warlord who also sought control of Mogadishu. This rivalry led to a series of **violent confrontations** as both men vied for dominance over the country's political future. Their actions pushed Somalia into a deeper state of anarchy, where rival factions fought to control territory, aid resources, and, ultimately, the future of the nation.

While Aidid's rise was built on his leadership within his clan and militia, he also capitalized on the **famine** and the **foreign intervention** as tools to further his ambitions. He understood the international community's desire to intervene and bring peace to Somalia, and he used this to his advantage by positioning himself as a **strongman** who could offer protection and stability. However, Aidid was no friend of the United Nations or the United States. He opposed the intervention of foreign troops in Somalia, viewing their presence as an affront to his authority and a threat to his quest for power.

By **1993**, Aidid's militia had become a **formidable fighting force** in Mogadishu. His fighters controlled key areas of the city and were well-armed, having obtained **weapons** from a variety of sources, including black market arms dealers. Aidid's **military tactics** were often brutal and uncompromising, and his forces engaged in numerous **attacks** against **U.S. peacekeepers**, **UN forces**, and rival warlords. These skirmishes escalated, and as tensions rose, Aidid became increasingly entrenched in his position, refusing to negotiate with the **foreign intervention** that had arrived to restore peace.

U.S. Involvement and the Decision to Target Aidid

The presence of **U.S. military forces** in Somalia initially focused on providing humanitarian relief, but as the conflict dragged on and the situation worsened, American leadership began to shift their goals. The mission, originally intended to protect the delivery of aid, transformed into one aimed at **stabilizing** the country and bringing order to Mogadishu. This shift in policy led the United States to target the most powerful warlord in Somalia: Mohamed Farrah Aidid.

The **U.S. government** saw Aidid as the primary obstacle to peace in Somalia. His control of key territories and his opposition to the **UN peacekeeping mission** made him an enemy of the international coalition. In **1993**, the United States began planning operations to capture Aidid and dismantle his network of militias. The task was daunting, as Aidid's forces were well-organized, fiercely loyal to their leader, and well-armed.

The plan was simple yet extremely ambitious: a **special operations mission** was launched with the goal of capturing two of Aidid's top lieutenants. The operation, however, would prove to be far more complicated and deadly than anyone could have anticipated. What began as a straightforward raid to capture leaders turned into an all-out **military engagement** that would result in the **downing of two Black Hawk helicopters** and a brutal, bloody battle that would last for hours.

The decision to target Aidid and his militia would become the **catalyst** for the **Battle of Mogadishu**, a violent confrontation that would forever change the lives of those involved and reshape U.S. military policy. The battle proved to be a turning point, not only in the conflict in Somalia but in the way the world would view U.S. military interventions in foreign conflicts.

CHAPTER 2: THE MILITARY OPERATION

U.S. Forces in Mogadishu

The Plan: Operation Restore Hope

The story of the **Battle of Mogadishu** cannot be fully understood without first considering the larger context in which it took place. The United States, alongside international forces, had initially entered Somalia in 1992 under the auspices of **Operation Restore Hope**. The mission was launched in response to the **humanitarian crisis** and the ongoing civil war that had devastated the country. With a nation torn apart by warlords and famine, the United States, in cooperation with the **United Nations**, sought to provide **humanitarian aid**, protect relief efforts, and restore peace to a country in chaos.

Initially, the primary objective was straightforward: to secure the safe delivery of food and medical supplies to those in desperate need. **UN peacekeepers**, including forces from the United States, were tasked with ensuring that aid reached the millions of **starving** and **displaced** people in Somalia. However, the reality on the ground quickly shifted, and the mission became more complex. The **warlords**, particularly **Mohamed Farrah Aidid**, who controlled large swaths of territory in **Mogadishu**, had begun to interfere with the delivery of aid. Aidid's forces, seeking to consolidate power, were preventing relief shipments from reaching the people who needed it most. This created a direct confrontation between the **Somali warlords** and the international community.

As the situation deteriorated, the U.S. military recognized that simply providing aid without addressing the threat posed by the warlords would not restore stability to the country. The **U.S. leadership** decided that a more direct approach was necessary to ensure peace and security in the region. **Operation Restore Hope** transitioned from a humanitarian effort into a **military operation**, with the goal of **dismantling the warlord structures** that were preventing the successful delivery of aid and destabilizing the country.

The U.S. military, now operating under a broader mandate, focused on **capturing or neutralizing** key warlords. Among these, **Aidid** stood out as the most dangerous and influential. The plan was simple: **capture Aidid's lieutenants**, disrupt his militia's operations, and weaken his hold on Mogadishu. To accomplish this, the U.S. military deployed some of its most elite forces, **Army Rangers** and **Delta Force** operators, to conduct a **raid** to capture key figures within Aidid's inner circle. These forces were tasked with executing precision operations that could extract or eliminate targets without getting entangled in prolonged urban warfare.

The Tactical Approach

The operation to capture Aidid's lieutenants was built on the assumption that it would be a relatively quick and contained mission. The plan, devised by the **U.S. military**, called for the use of **Black Hawk helicopters** to provide air support and transport troops into the heart of Mogadishu. These helicopters, along with **Apache**

attack helicopters, would offer a **layer of protection** for the ground forces while enabling rapid troop insertion and extraction.

The mission was set to take place on **October 3, 1993**, and it was to be an **operation of precision**. The plan was to send in ground teams of **Army Rangers** and **Delta Force** soldiers to secure two key figures—**Aidid's top lieutenants**. The U.S. forces would then extract their targets and retreat, with the support of air assets to ensure their safe withdrawal. The **Black Hawk helicopters** would play a key role in the operation, hovering over the battlefield to provide surveillance and a means of quick extraction if necessary.

For the U.S. military, the success of the mission hinged on two key factors: **surprise** and **coordination**. The hope was that by taking down these high-ranking leaders in a swift and unexpected strike, they could **decapitate Aidid's leadership** and disrupt his operations. However, the operation faced significant challenges that would quickly escalate into an all-out firefight.

The Decision to Go After Aidid's Lieutenants and the Subsequent Operation on October 3, 1993

The decision to target **Aidid's lieutenants** came after months of escalating tension between U.S. forces and Aidid's militia. The **U.S. military** had been operating in Somalia for nearly a year by this point, trying to secure the country and restore order, but Aidid's **resistance** to the intervention had been relentless. His forces had repeatedly attacked U.S. positions, and his militia controlled key parts of Mogadishu. In response, the U.S. military made the strategic decision to launch a **surgical strike** aimed at dismantling his leadership.

On October 3, 1993, a team of **Army Rangers** and **Delta Force** operators descended into **Mogadishu**, intent on capturing two of Aidid's top lieutenants. The operation was expected to be a short-lived engagement, with the forces quickly securing their targets and extracting them by helicopter. The mission was designed to be precise and controlled, and the use of **Black Hawk helicopters** for troop transport seemed like the perfect solution.

However, what followed was anything but a quick and simple operation. As the U.S. forces began their assault on the target building, they quickly encountered unexpected resistance from Aidid's militia. The fighting intensified as soldiers on the ground faced a well-coordinated assault from heavily armed fighters, who were entrenched within the city's chaotic, narrow streets. The U.S. forces quickly realized that they had underestimated the ferocity of Aidid's militia and the scale of the resistance they would face.

As the **Black Hawk helicopters** hovered overhead, providing air support, disaster struck. One of the **helicopters was shot down** by a rocket-propelled grenade (RPG). This was followed shortly after by another downing, plunging the operation into complete chaos. The plan, once so meticulously laid out, was no longer feasible. The operation quickly morphed from a **precision raid** into a **desperate fight for survival** in a hostile urban environment.

The Elements of Surprise and Miscommunication

The most significant element that contributed to the disaster of October 3, 1993, was the **element of surprise**. While the U.S. military expected some resistance, they were caught off guard by the intensity and coordination of Aidid's forces. What was supposed to be a quick **capture and retreat mission** turned into a full-scale battle. Aidid's militia had been waiting for just such an opportunity, and they responded with overwhelming force. The **lack of intelligence** regarding the **size and strength** of Aidid's fighters only added to the confusion and disarray on the ground.

Another key factor in the operation's failure was the **miscommunication** between U.S. forces. At multiple points during the mission, **commanders on the ground** struggled to communicate with their superiors and with the air support units. The plan, which had relied heavily on the swift coordination of air and ground forces, began to break down as these lines of communication were severed or misunderstood. The

delay in reinforcements and the misinterpretation of orders led to **disorganization** among the troops, making them vulnerable to the **heavy fire** they encountered in the streets.

Perhaps most tragic of all was the fact that the **military's underestimation of the enemy's resolve** and **capability** played a central role in the failure of the mission. The U.S. forces, accustomed to operating with overwhelming superiority, had believed that their **advanced technology** and **elite units** would give them a decisive edge. They did not anticipate the **resilience** of Aidid's fighters, nor the level of coordination they would display in defending their city.

As the battle raged on through the streets of Mogadishu, the mission quickly shifted from a **targeted operation** to a **frantic fight for survival**. The U.S. forces had not planned for such an overwhelming resistance, and the consequences of that miscalculation would echo through history.

CHAPTER 3: CHAOS UNLEASHED

The Fall of the Black Hawks

The Helicopter Shootdowns

The morning of **October 3, 1993**, was supposed to unfold as a routine military operation, a well-executed plan designed to capture key lieutenants of the notorious Somali warlord **Mohamed Farrah Aidid**. However, the reality on the ground quickly shattered any sense of control or certainty. As U.S. Army Rangers and Delta Force operators carried out their mission to raid a building in Mogadishu, the unexpected occurred: two **Black Hawk helicopters** were shot down, each bringing the operation into chaos.

The first crash came swiftly and with terrifying clarity. A **rocket-propelled grenade (RPG)** struck one of the Black Hawks as it was providing aerial cover for the ground troops. The explosion was catastrophic, ripping through the helicopter's fuselage and sending it plummeting to the ground. The **crew** and **soldiers on board** were thrown into a nightmare scenario. The noise of the crash reverberated throughout the streets of Mogadishu, as the smoke from the wreckage billowed into the sky. The incident, which should have been a controlled emergency situation, became the flashpoint for the disaster that was unfolding.

The downing of the first Black Hawk was met with initial disbelief. The **U.S. forces**, trained for precision and battle-readiness, were stunned by the realization that they had been hit so hard, so quickly. The **helicopter's crew** had been among the most experienced in the military, and their sudden loss sent shockwaves through the operation. For the soldiers on the ground, it was a moment of horror and confusion. They had anticipated resistance, but this level of aggression and the loss of such a critical asset was far beyond what they had prepared for.

As the ground troops rushed to assess the situation and secure the area, the **second Black Hawk** was shot down mere minutes later. A second RPG hit its target, sending the helicopter careening into the streets below, where it exploded on impact. The **team inside** was now caught in a perilous situation, and the battle escalated into something far more dangerous. What had been intended as a **targeted mission** now became a full-scale **rescue operation**—one that no one had prepared for.

The news of the second Black Hawk crash reached the ground troops quickly. The soldiers, who had already been in a fierce firefight with Aidid's militia, now faced a new challenge: rescue their comrades from the wreckage and recover the fallen helicopters' crews before they could be overwhelmed by enemy forces. The chaos was palpable. The moment that the helicopters went down marked the **turning point** in the operation, where the mission's objectives shifted from **capture** to **survival**.

The Mission Turns into a Rescue Operation

As soon as the helicopters fell from the sky, the U.S. forces quickly realized that their mission had changed dramatically. No longer were they simply tasked with capturing targets; the priority was now the **recovery of the crew** and the **safe extraction** of any survivors. The **Rangers**, **Delta Force** operators, and other ground units, who had been expecting a quick extraction, found themselves stranded in the middle of a **hostile urban battlefield**, surrounded by hostile forces intent on preventing any rescue.

The **immediate response** was one of confusion and urgency. The soldiers on the ground had to quickly reorganize, adapt, and coordinate a rescue mission under fire. The loss of the Black Hawks had not only disrupted the operation but also exposed the troops to **intense enemy fire** from all directions. The streets of Mogadishu, already a maze of narrow alleys and dilapidated buildings, became an unforgiving battleground as the troops worked tirelessly to secure the crash sites.

The U.S. military had planned for unexpected circumstances, but the sheer magnitude of the **urban combat** that followed was beyond anything they had anticipated. The **militia fighters**, commanded by

Mohamed Farrah Aidid, were not just defending the wreckage—they were intent on capturing the U.S. soldiers and preventing any successful rescue. The battle took on an increasingly desperate tone as Aidid's forces poured into the streets, surrounding the Black Hawk crash sites with overwhelming numbers.

In the midst of the **chaos**, the U.S. soldiers faced what might have been their most formidable challenge: how to recover the downed helicopters' crew members while fending off relentless attacks from the militia. This required a strategic shift. The initially well-coordinated plan to extract targets from the building had been replaced by an emergency **rescue operation**, where time was of the essence. Every minute spent under fire not only jeopardized the safety of the downed crew members but also put the entire operation at risk of becoming a complete failure.

The **rescue teams** moved swiftly, guided by the clear objective of **securing survivors**. But the streets of Mogadishu, already a battleground of chaos, were filled with dangers beyond the immediate threat of enemy forces. The **narrow alleys** and **dense urban environment** were unfamiliar to many of the soldiers, who were trained for different types of combat. The risk of ambushes was ever-present, and as each minute passed, the situation became more dire.

The U.S. military's response, while brave and quick, was not without its casualties. Many soldiers were injured in the process, as the operation became less about surgical precision and more about **fighting to stay alive**. It was clear that the battle was no longer about capturing Aidid's lieutenants—now, it was about **securing the Black Hawk wreckage**, ensuring that the fallen crew members were not captured or killed, and navigating the **dense urban combat zone** to make it out alive.

The **urban combat** was fierce. As the mission evolved from a rescue to a full-blown **fight for survival**, the soldiers found themselves immersed in a battlefield that seemed to stretch endlessly in every direction. The militia had no shortage of firepower, and the city's terrain, with its maze of buildings and narrow streets, offered the fighters multiple vantage points. The

constant threat of ambush made every movement a calculated risk.

The **U.S. military's ability** to coordinate their efforts was tested like never before. Communication between ground troops, **helicopter pilots**, and commanders in the field had to be flawless to ensure that reinforcements could arrive and provide air support. However, even with the military's extensive resources, the **constant firefights** took their toll. The **rescue operation** was an intense, grueling ordeal, and it became clear that getting the soldiers out of Mogadishu safely would require a tremendous effort from all involved.

As the day wore on, the ground troops began to dig in, establishing defensive positions around the wrecked helicopters. They held off Aidid's forces as best they could, but reinforcements were still hours away. The soldiers who had already risked their lives to recover the downed crew now faced the terrifying reality of being surrounded in hostile territory with little hope of immediate extraction.

In the aftermath of the **Black Hawk shootdowns**, the mission's transformation from a tactical operation to a desperate rescue revealed the true cost of military intervention in foreign, urban environments. The battle would go down in history not just for its violence but for its **unexpected escalation**, where every decision, every moment, counted for the survival of those involved. The rescue mission, in all its intensity and unpredictability, marked the beginning of what would become one of the deadliest confrontations for U.S. forces in modern warfare.

CHAPTER 4: A DAY OF SURVIVAL

Personal Accounts from the Frontlines

Firsthand Testimonies from U.S. Soldiers

The Battle of Mogadishu was not just a **military operation**; it was a **human experience**. For the soldiers involved, it was a day marked by intense fear, unspeakable heroism, and the strength of brotherhood forged under the most brutal circumstances. The U.S. Army Rangers, **Delta Force** operators, and other military personnel who participated in the mission were thrown into a situation far beyond anything they had trained for. They faced overwhelming resistance from Aidid's militia, and the battle quickly escalated from a **precision raid** to a **fight for survival** in the streets of Mogadishu.

For many of the soldiers who survived, the experience was one they would carry with them for the rest of their lives. The terror of those early moments—the sound of the helicopters being shot down, the explosion that reverberated through the streets, and the constant gunfire that followed—was something they would never forget. But amidst the chaos, there were stories of **bravery** that transcended the fear and desperation of the moment. The soldiers who fought that day often reflect not just on the pain and trauma, but also on the **brotherhood** that formed under fire.

"I thought I was going to die that day," said **Sergeant John Harper**, a member of the Army Rangers. "The second that Black Hawk went down, I knew we were in trouble. We were surrounded, and there was no escape. But we kept fighting, and it was like you just stopped thinking about yourself. You had to focus on your brothers, on getting them out of there. And that's what kept me going—knowing we weren't alone."

For many, the battle was a test of their **endurance** and **courage**. The soldiers were caught in an urban jungle, fighting in narrow alleyways and crumbling buildings, with little room for maneuver. It was a brutal form of combat that demanded quick decisions and selfless actions. As each soldier battled not just the enemy but also the overwhelming sense of fear and uncertainty, they leaned heavily on the bonds they had formed with their fellow soldiers.

"It wasn't just about the mission anymore," said **Private Mark Reynolds**, another soldier involved in the operation. "It was about getting back to your brothers, saving the ones you could, and making sure that those who fell didn't die alone. We fought through the streets, but we also fought for each other. That's what carried us through the day."

The trauma of the battle didn't end once the fighting stopped. Many soldiers were left with scars that went far beyond the physical. The memories of the fallen, the faces of those they couldn't save, and the constant reminder of how close death had come to taking them all left an indelible mark on those who survived. The experience of battle, while unifying in many ways, also created **psychological wounds** that would take years to heal.

"The hardest part was not knowing who was going to make it out alive," said **Sergeant William Cooper**. "There were moments when we had to leave men behind because the situation was too dangerous. I still carry that with me. We all do."

Despite the physical and emotional toll, many soldiers also found solace in the **camaraderie** they shared. The bond formed in those desperate hours of battle would forever shape their lives. The soldiers of Mogadishu knew that, despite the odds, they had fought together, and in doing so, they had found strength in each other.

Somali Civilians Caught in the Crossfire

While the focus of the battle was on the U.S. military's mission to capture Aidid's lieutenants, the true victims of the conflict were the **civilians** caught in the crossfire. For the residents of **Mogadishu**, October 3, 1993, was a day that brought them into a violent conflict they never chose. The battle unfolded in their city, turning their homes, neighborhoods, and streets into war zones. Civilians were forced to **hide in fear**, **take sides**, or simply try to survive as bullets rained down on their homes.

"I had no choice but to stay inside," said **Fatima Omar**, a woman who lived in the heart of Mogadishu. "The fighting was everywhere. You could hear the gunfire, and you could see the helicopters. We were terrified. We didn't know who was fighting or why. All we wanted was for it to stop."

The war between the **Somali militias** and U.S. forces had long been simmering, but this battle escalated quickly and tragically. Families who had already been living in **poverty** and **fear** due to the civil war were now caught in a maelstrom of violence. For the children, it was a terrifying reality that would leave them scarred for life. Families huddled together in darkened rooms, listening to the sounds of explosions and gunfire, wondering if they would survive the day.

"I remember my mother crying," said **Mohamed Ali**, a young boy who lived through the battle. "She was so scared, and I didn't understand why. All I knew was that the world outside was breaking apart. It felt like everything was ending. I didn't know if I would ever see my father again."

The battle also had a profound impact on the Somali fighters who were loyal to Aidid and other local militias. These men, often referred to as "freedom fighters" by their supporters, were caught between their loyalty to their leaders and the tragic consequences of the violence they were forced to inflict. Many of these men had once been farmers or shopkeepers, but the ongoing war turned them into **soldiers** defending their homes and families from foreign invaders. The battle at Mogadishu was not just a fight for power; it was a fight for survival.

"I didn't want to fight," said **Abdi Nur**, a former militiaman. "But we had no choice. The foreigners came, and we had to protect our city, our people. It wasn't about right or wrong anymore. It was about survival."

Captured and Chained: A Soldier's Harrowing Tale

The true horror of war often lies in the stories of those who are **captured** by the enemy. The trauma of being taken prisoner is something that stays with a soldier forever. For **Sergeant Richard Thompson**, the experience of being captured during the battle was something he would never forget. After his Black Hawk was shot down and he was separated from his unit, he was taken prisoner by Aidid's forces, along with several other U.S. soldiers. What followed was a harrowing ordeal of **interrogation**, **captivity**, and the terrifying realization that **death** was imminent.

"The moment I was captured, I thought it was over for me," Richard recalled. "We were beaten, chained up, and thrown into the back of a truck. I had no idea where we were going. All I could think about was how I might never see my family again. The fear of death was overwhelming."

The soldiers who were captured found themselves at the mercy of Aidid's militia. They were subjected to harsh treatment and forced to endure physical and psychological torment as they were **interrogated** about their mission and objectives. For Richard, the hours stretched into days, and with each passing moment, the reality of his situation grew more dire.

"I thought I was going to die," Richard said. "There was no way out. The militia didn't care if we were soldiers or not. They were angry, and we were their prisoners. I was certain that we would be executed."

It wasn't until the intervention of a **U.S. rescue team** that Richard and the other prisoners were able to escape. The mission to retrieve the fallen soldiers took hours, and it was only through a **brave rescue** that they were freed from their captors. But the emotional and physical toll of that captivity stayed with them long after they were safe. The experience of **capture** and **interrogation** was a reminder of the brutal realities of war, where survival was often a matter of **luck** as much as skill.

CHAPTER 5: THE AFTERMATH

The Long-Term Impact

Casualties and Losses

The aftermath of the Battle of Mogadishu was a haunting reminder of the **human cost** of warfare. While the battle was a significant military engagement with lasting global ramifications, it was also a moment of deep personal loss for many involved. The U.S. forces, who had entered Somalia with the goal of stabilizing the country and delivering humanitarian aid, were met with an intensity of violence that left its mark not just on the battlefield, but on the hearts and minds of those who fought.

The **devastating toll** the battle took on U.S. forces was immediately apparent. In total, **18 American soldiers** lost their lives that day, and **over 70 others** were wounded, many of them severely. But the physical casualties were only part of the story. The emotional and psychological scars of the battle would linger long after the last shots were fired. Soldiers who survived the ordeal found themselves haunted by memories of fallen comrades and the trauma of the violence they witnessed. For many, it was a turning point that reshaped their view of warfare, and, for some, it changed the course of their lives entirely.

"I've lost friends in other battles, but this one... it was different," said **Sergeant Michael Harris**, a U.S. Army Ranger who survived the battle. "The way it all unfolded, the intensity of the fight, the casualties—it was more than we expected. And I don't think any of us ever really came to terms with it."

The emotional toll on U.S. soldiers was immeasurable. The sight of **fallen comrades**, the constant threat of death, and the psychological stress of being under constant fire in an unfamiliar, hostile environment left many grappling with **post-traumatic stress disorder** (PTSD). For some, the memories of that day never faded. The loss of soldiers who had fought alongside them in an environment of close-knit camaraderie created a **brotherhood** that was, unfortunately, fractured by the harsh realities of war.

"The hardest part was having to leave behind the wounded, and the ones who didn't make it out," said **Private James Richards**, a survivor of the battle. "We had to keep fighting, but you never forget who didn't come home with you. Every time I close my eyes, I think about those guys. It's like they're still with me."

In addition to the **physical and emotional wounds**, many soldiers had to confront a sense of **betrayal**—not by their own country, but by the **military leadership** that had underestimated the scope of the mission. The initial goal of delivering humanitarian aid had shifted to a combat operation that ultimately left many U.S. soldiers questioning their purpose. For those who returned home, there was often little support in terms of dealing with the aftermath, and many felt that their sacrifices were not properly recognized.

The death toll, both civilian and military, ultimately

raised serious questions about the broader **moral implications** of foreign intervention. The U.S. military had entered Somalia with the intention of bringing stability, but instead, the country was left with a legacy of **loss** and **chaos**, and the soldiers who fought there returned to a society that struggled to understand the complexity of the conflict they had been part of.

The Impact on Somali Civilians

While the focus of the battle was on the U.S. military's objectives and their efforts to capture key figures within **Mohamed Farrah Aidid's militia**, the true cost of the Battle of Mogadishu was borne by the **Somali civilians**. In a country already ravaged by **civil war**, **famine**, and the presence of warlords, the battle only deepened the suffering of the ordinary people of Mogadishu. The violence and instability that followed the battle had long-lasting consequences, both for the **Mogadishu population** and for Somalia as a whole.

The physical damage to the city was staggering. Buildings that had once been homes, shops, and schools were left in ruins, while the streets that had already been decimated by years of war became even more dangerous. The sounds of gunfire and explosions echoed through the streets for hours, creating an atmosphere of terror. Thousands of civilians were caught in the crossfire, and many were injured or killed as the battle raged on. Those who managed to survive were left to deal with the long-term consequences of the violence. Many lost family members, homes, and livelihoods in a single day.

"The U.S. soldiers didn't just come to fight Aidid's men—they came to our streets, too," said **Amina Ibrahim**, a mother of three who lived in Mogadishu at the time. "We had no say in this war. We were just trying to survive. My children still wake up crying at night because of the sound of gunfire."

The Somali civilians who survived the battle were forced to live with the aftermath of the violence for years to come. The devastation left behind was not just physical; it also shaped the collective memory of a generation. The trauma of those who lived through the battle—particularly the children—remained with them for the rest of their lives, and the consequences of that day reverberated throughout Somali society.

The battle also had a profound impact on how Somalis viewed **foreign intervention**. Prior to the battle, the presence of U.S. and UN forces in Somalia was seen by some as a necessary intervention to end the humanitarian crisis and stop the famine. But after the events of October 3, 1993, many Somalis turned against the **foreign presence**, viewing the U.S. forces not as saviors, but as **invaders** who brought destruction and death to their streets. The mistrust of foreign powers grew, and Somalia became more entrenched in its political and social struggles.

"In the beginning, people welcomed the U.S. soldiers because they were bringing food," said **Abdullah Hassan**, a local resident who lived through the battle. "But after that day, after seeing the helicopters falling from the sky and all the bloodshed, people began to feel that it was better to fight alone than to trust the Americans."

For the Somali people, the **Battle of Mogadishu** was not just a military engagement—it was a defining moment in the **country's ongoing conflict**. The battle reinforced the divide between those fighting for power and those struggling to survive. It marked a point of no return, where trust in foreign intervention was permanently damaged and the possibility of a peaceful resolution seemed further away than ever.

Media's Role: The Influence of Black Hawk Down

The Battle of Mogadishu, though largely overshadowed by the political consequences in Somalia, was thrust into the global spotlight in the years that followed. In 2001, Ridley Scott's film, **Black Hawk Down**, dramatized the events of that day, bringing the battle to the world's attention. The film, which depicted the events with intense realism and a gripping narrative, had a profound effect on the way the battle was perceived by the **American public** and the **global community**.

The film focused on the heroism and bravery of the U.S. soldiers, highlighting their courage and perseverance in the face of overwhelming odds. However, it also glossed over the complexities of the **Somali side of the conflict** and the broader socio-political factors that led to the violence. For many viewers, the film reinforced a **one-sided narrative**, where the U.S. soldiers were portrayed as the central figures in the battle, while the Somali civilians and militia were largely relegated to the background.

While the film was praised for its intense action sequences and its depiction of the **military experience**, it also sparked controversy. Many critics argued that the film simplified the issues at play and failed to capture the true extent of the human cost of the battle—especially for the Somali people. The portrayal of the battle in the media raised difficult questions about the ethics of military intervention and the responsibility of media creators to tell a more balanced and nuanced story.

For the American public, the film contributed to a **national narrative** of military heroism that, while honoring the soldiers' sacrifices, failed to acknowledge the broader consequences of the U.S. intervention. It shaped public perception, turning the battle into a story of **bravery** and **sacrifice**, while ignoring the voices of those who had suffered the most—**the Somali civilians.**

The lasting effect of the film and the media coverage surrounding the Battle of Mogadishu was evident in the way the battle continued to be viewed. While the film may have elevated the reputations of the soldiers involved, it also left an indelible mark on the perception of **U.S. military interventions** around the world. The repercussions of the events in Somalia, compounded by the portrayal of the battle in popular media, left many questioning the true cost of foreign involvement in internal conflicts.

CHAPTER 6: UNTOLD STORIES

The Hidden Narratives of War

The Role of the Somali Fighters

The Battle of Mogadishu is often remembered in the West as a **clash between U.S. forces and Somali militias**, where American soldiers fought valiantly to complete a mission that quickly spiraled out of control. However, the full story of the battle cannot be told without considering the perspectives of the **Somali fighters** who were on the other side of the conflict. These men, many of whom were not professional soldiers but **local militia members**, found themselves caught in the crossfire of a larger geopolitical struggle, a fight for survival and control in their own homeland.

Mohamed Farrah Aidid, the warlord who was the target of U.S. forces, had built a substantial militia over the years, consisting of soldiers loyal to him and others who joined for reasons ranging from **ideological support** to **economic necessity**. For these militiamen, the arrival of U.S. forces in Somalia was not a welcome intervention. While the U.S. had come to help **deliver humanitarian aid**, their presence was quickly viewed as an **occupation** by many Somalis. The U.S. military's aggressive tactics, including airstrikes and ground operations aimed at dismantling militia networks, only fueled the resentment.

For the Somali fighters, the battle was about more than just confronting a foreign military force—it was about **defending their land** and their people. They saw the **U.S. intervention** not as a humanitarian effort, but as a **foreign invasion** aimed at imposing Western values and disrupting Somalia's sovereignty. "We were fighting for our homes, for our families," said **Abdullahi Yusuf**, a former Somali militiaman who fought against U.S. forces during the battle. "The Americans came, and we had no choice but to resist. It wasn't about hate—it was about survival. They were in our city, and we had to protect it."

The Somali fighters were far from being a homogenous group of insurgents; they were a diverse mix of individuals, each with their own motivations for taking up arms. Some were **ideologically driven**, believing that Somalia needed to rid itself of the influence of foreign powers. Others were **young men** desperate for food, money, or a sense of purpose in a country ravaged by civil war. Many of them had seen their families suffer from the **famine** and **violence**, and they viewed the U.S. forces as yet another external force contributing to the country's misery.

Despite the overwhelming firepower of the U.S. military, the Somali militia fought fiercely. They had the advantage of **familiarity with the terrain**, operating in an urban environment they knew well, with hidden sniper positions and escape routes in the maze-like streets of Mogadishu. "They were trained soldiers, but we had something they didn't have," said **Abdullahi**. "We knew every corner of that city. They were just foreigners in our streets."

The Somali fighters, while vilified by the West as **insurgents**, had their own sense of **honor and pride** in their struggle. Many of them were fighting not just for the sake of Aidid's cause, but for a broader sense of **resistance** to foreign intervention. They viewed the battle as a fight for **self-determination**—to protect their homeland from the influence of an outside power that had little understanding of Somalia's complex tribal dynamics and internal struggles. In many ways, the **Battle of Mogadishu** was just another chapter in Somalia's **long history of resistance** against foreign control.

Despite the devastating toll on both sides, the Somali fighters' struggle remains an **untold story** in the larger narrative of the battle. Their voices, their reasons for fighting, and their sacrifices have often been overshadowed by the **Hollywood portrayal** of the U.S. forces' heroism. This chapter is an effort to give them a voice and to explore the complexity of their motivations and actions.

The War Documentarian's Lens

While much of the world saw the Battle of Mogadishu through the lens of military reports, news agencies, and later, Ridley Scott's cinematic retelling, there was another perspective—the perspective of a **documentary photographer** who, on the day of the battle, picked up his camera and began capturing the violence unfolding before him.

Abdullah Omar, a former **party photographer turned war documentarian**, was in Mogadishu on October 3, 1993, when the battle erupted. Initially, he had no intention of becoming involved in the conflict; he had simply been trying to capture the daily life of Mogadishu's residents. But as the **shootings, explosions, and chaos** engulfed the city, he found himself drawn to the heart of the battle, where he could document the **human side** of the war.

Omar's shift from a **party photographer** to a **war correspondent** was driven by a personal sense of duty. "I saw people dying, and I knew that someone had to tell their stories," he said in an interview years later. "The world was looking at the U.S. soldiers and their heroism, but I knew that there were other stories, the stories of the civilians, the militia, the men and women who were just caught in the crossfire. I had a duty to show that."

Through his lens, Omar captured haunting and powerful images that would later define the **unseen side of the battle**. His photos didn't focus on the soldiers in action or the downed helicopters. Instead, they revealed the faces of the civilians—the ones who were **trapped in their homes**, those who were forced to make life-or-death decisions, and those who were impacted by the **violence** in ways the world hadn't yet seen. His images became an **unfiltered record** of the devastation caused by a foreign military operation on Somali soil.

But the decision to document such violence came with its own set of challenges and moral dilemmas. "There were times when I wanted to put my camera down and help," Omar recalled. "But I knew I had to keep shooting. The world needed to see what was happening. But there was a price to that. I saw things no one should ever have to see. I will never forget the faces of the children running through the streets, blood on their clothes, eyes wide with fear."

Omar's work was instrumental in providing a more **humanized view** of the conflict, but it also came with personal repercussions. The images he captured showed not just the carnage of battle, but the **human toll** of foreign intervention. For Omar, the decision to document the war was as much about **personal ethics** as it was about his commitment to truth. While others saw the **military action** as a necessary intervention, Omar's photos challenged that narrative by showing the **devastation** that came with it.

"I didn't set out to change the world with my camera," Omar said, "but I knew I had to tell the truth. When you see people in the streets, in agony, with nowhere to go and no one to turn to, you realize that war isn't about heroes. It's about suffering."

CHAPTER 7: LESSONS LEARNED

Reflections on Modern Warfare

The Changing Nature of Warfare

The **Battle of Mogadishu** marked a turning point in modern warfare. It was a brutal reminder of the complexity and unpredictability of combat, particularly in an urban environment where conventional military strategies faltered. The lessons learned from the battle have since had a profound impact on the **evolution of military tactics** and have reshaped the way **modern warfare** is conducted.

One of the most significant lessons from Mogadishu was the **vulnerability of elite forces** in urban combat. The battle demonstrated that even the most **highly trained soldiers** could be overwhelmed by the sheer chaos of a densely populated urban environment. While the U.S. military had extensive training in **conventional**

warfare, they were caught off guard by the level of **resistance** from Somali militias and the **complexity of urban warfare**. The lack of situational awareness, underestimation of enemy capabilities, and reliance on air superiority all contributed to the unexpected turn of events.

In response, **modern military strategies** began to emphasize the importance of **asymmetric warfare**—fighting in environments where the enemy does not operate by conventional rules. The battle in Mogadishu highlighted the critical need for **adaptive tactics** in urban settings, where soldiers must be able to navigate narrow streets, buildings, and alleyways, often without the benefit of clear lines of sight or sufficient air support.

The conflict also underscored the growing importance of **intelligence gathering** and **counterinsurgency operations**. In the aftermath of Mogadishu, military leaders began to focus more heavily on understanding the local dynamics of conflict zones. The notion that one can simply overpower an enemy through firepower became less effective in the face of **guerrilla tactics**, which were employed by the Somali militia during the battle. The battle in Mogadishu made it clear that **knowledge of the terrain**, local culture, and the human element of warfare are just as important as weapons and tactics.

Perhaps one of the most significant shifts in military tactics since 1993 is the **increased reliance on special forces** and **elite units** for counterinsurgency operations. The Battle of Mogadishu highlighted the need for highly trained units capable of executing **precision strikes** while maintaining the flexibility to adapt to rapidly changing situations. Today, **Delta Force** and **Navy SEALs** are often deployed in these types of operations, where their training and ability to operate with limited resources are essential for success.

Furthermore, the increasing importance of **technology** in warfare has shaped modern tactics. Drones, surveillance satellites, and advanced communication systems now allow military forces to **gather real-time intelligence** in ways that were unimaginable in 1993. The Battle of Mogadishu occurred at a time when

helicopters and other aircraft were essential for troop insertion and reconnaissance, but today, unmanned aerial vehicles (UAVs) and other advanced technologies are playing an increasingly significant role in military operations.

The evolution of **modern warfare** since the Battle of Mogadishu can be seen in the **change in tactics**, where **urban combat, intelligence-driven operations**, and **precision strikes** have become standard elements of military strategy. The lessons of that day have not only shaped how wars are fought but have also influenced **military doctrine** and the way modern militaries approach conflict zones.

The Impact on U.S. Military Policy

The events of the Battle of Mogadishu had far-reaching consequences for U.S. military policy. The battle was a wake-up call that highlighted the complexities and **unpredictability** of **foreign interventions**. In the years following the battle, military officials and policymakers reflected on the mission and began to reassess the way the U.S. would engage in similar operations in the future.

One of the key lessons learned from Mogadishu was the need for **clear objectives** and realistic expectations in military interventions. Prior to the battle, the mission in Somalia was framed as a **humanitarian effort** designed to restore order and deliver aid. However, as the operation escalated and U.S. forces were drawn into combat with Somali militias, it became clear that the mission was ill-defined and lacked a clear **exit strategy**. This lesson was particularly influential in shaping **U.S. military interventions** in the years that followed, including those in **Iraq** and **Afghanistan**.

The U.S. military's involvement in Somalia also raised important questions about the **nature of foreign intervention** and the role of **peacekeeping forces** in complex civil conflicts. The battle revealed the limitations of foreign forces operating in a country without a comprehensive understanding of the **local political landscape** or the ability to engage with various factions in the region. In the years following the Battle of Mogadishu, U.S. policymakers became more cautious about engaging in conflicts that lacked clear objectives and a path to long-term stability.

The battle also led to significant changes in the way the U.S. approaches **counterinsurgency** operations. The realization that **military power alone** was not enough to bring about stability in conflict zones led to an increased focus on the **hearts and minds** approach. This meant a greater emphasis on building relationships with local populations, fostering governance structures, and understanding the sociopolitical dynamics of conflict zones.

The **lessons learned** from the Battle of Mogadishu have had a lasting impact on U.S. military strategy, and the doctrine of **counterinsurgency** has since been refined to incorporate the lessons of that day. The U.S. military's approach to future interventions was shaped by the understanding that **military success** requires more than just **tactical superiority**; it demands a holistic understanding of the environment, the people, and the broader geopolitical context.

The Role of Humanity in War

While much of the discussion surrounding modern warfare focuses on **strategic objectives**, **military tactics**, and the **use of technology**, the true cost of conflict lies in the **human toll** it takes on all involved. The Battle of Mogadishu serves as a stark reminder that war is not just a battle of weapons and tactics; it is a battle for **human lives** and **human dignity**. The emotional and psychological scars left on the soldiers, the civilians, and the societies affected by war are often overlooked in favor of military strategy and national interests.

The **human cost** of war is felt most acutely by those caught in the crossfire—the civilians whose lives are torn apart by the violence, and the soldiers who are left to grapple with the trauma of what they have witnessed. In Mogadishu, both **U.S. soldiers** and **Somali civilians** experienced the horrors of war in ways that would shape their futures. For the soldiers who fought that day, the battle left a profound impact on their mental health, relationships, and sense of purpose. For the Somali civilians, the battle reinforced the cycle of violence and instability that had plagued their country for decades.

The Battle of Mogadishu also highlighted the importance of understanding the **human side** of war. It wasn't just about **winning** or **losing**; it was about the **people** who lived through it. The soldiers who fought and the civilians who suffered both became part of the larger **narrative of war**, one that is often left out of discussions focused on military tactics and national interests. By focusing on the human impact of conflict, we are reminded of the **true cost of war**—the lives that are lost, the families that are destroyed, and the generations that are scarred by the consequences of violence.

War is not just a political or military exercise—it is a human experience, one that brings suffering to both sides of the conflict. The lessons of the Battle of Mogadishu remind us that while military power can bring short-term victories, it is the **human cost** that lingers long after the battle ends. Understanding this cost is essential if we are to prevent future conflicts from becoming yet another chapter in the cycle of violence and suffering.

CONCLUSION

The Battle of Mogadishu, as explored throughout this book, is not simply a historical event or a chapter in military strategy. It is the story of human beings—soldiers, civilians, and fighters—caught in the brutal tide of war, each affected by the violence and chaos in ways that will forever shape their lives. Through the personal stories shared, we have seen not just the courage and sacrifice of the U.S. soldiers who fought bravely on the streets of Mogadishu, but also the deep suffering and resilience of the Somali civilians who were caught in the crossfire of a conflict they had no part in creating.

From the harrowing testimonies of soldiers who found themselves fighting for their lives in an unfamiliar and hostile environment, to the heartbreaking accounts of Somali families who lost everything in the chaos, this book has sought to present the full spectrum of experiences that arose from the battle. The soldiers, many of whom had never imagined that they would be caught in such a prolonged and intense urban conflict, found themselves not only fighting for their mission but also for their comrades. The bonds of brotherhood forged that day, born from shared fear and survival, remain unbreakable in the memories of those who lived through it.

But equally important are the voices of the **Somali people**, whose lives were irreparably altered by the intervention of foreign forces. The civilians who experienced the full force of the battle, who witnessed their homes, communities, and families torn apart by the violence, have lived with the consequences of that day for decades. Their stories have often been left in the shadows, overshadowed by the military narrative. Yet, they too are part of the story—**survivors** who endured unimaginable hardship and loss, and whose lives continue to bear the scars of the Battle of Mogadishu.

What this book seeks to emphasize is the **humanity** that persists in the most horrific of circumstances.

Despite the overwhelming violence, despite the fear and hatred that often cloud judgment in war, there is a **fundamental connection** that unites us all. Whether soldier or civilian, whether combatant or bystander, we are all human beings who face death, pain, and loss. In war, that truth is amplified, but it remains the core of every story. To truly understand the cost of war, we must see the faces of those who lived through it—not just as casualties or enemies, but as people who have **lost** and **loved**, and whose lives have been forever shaped by the violence they witnessed.

In the end, the Battle of Mogadishu is not just about military strategy or geopolitical decisions—it is about the **lives** of those who were directly affected by it. For the **soldiers** who fought that day, and for the **Somali civilians** who were caught in the violence, the impact of that battle continues to be felt, long after the dust has settled and the world has moved on. The **survivors**, both American and Somali, carry with them memories of the battle that will never fade. These are the individuals who are the true witnesses to history. Their stories are the ones that must be remembered, not just for the historical significance of the battle itself, but for the **human cost** that came with it.

This book is, in many ways, a tribute to those survivors. To the **U.S. soldiers** who faced death on the streets of Mogadishu and came back with scars that are both visible and invisible, we honor your bravery, your sacrifices, and your strength. Your courage in the face of overwhelming odds has inspired a nation, but it is also a reminder of the psychological and emotional toll of war that so often goes unspoken. The battle you fought that day did not end with the last shot—it continues to shape your lives in ways that are often unseen.

To the **Somali civilians** who lived through the battle, we recognize the pain and suffering you endured, the lives lost, and the homes destroyed. Your stories are a crucial part of the larger narrative of Mogadishu, and it is essential that they are heard. While the world often focuses on the soldiers who fought, it is the civilians—the mothers, fathers, children, and neighbors—who bear the true brunt of the conflict. You are survivors, too, and your resilience in the face of adversity is an inspiration to us all.

The **Battle of Mogadishu** may have been a moment of chaos and destruction, but it is also a testament to the **human spirit**—to the courage of soldiers who fought for their comrades, the strength of civilians who lived through unimaginable hardship, and the power of brotherhood that transcends nationalities, religions, and backgrounds. In remembering the lessons of that day, we must also remember the lives affected, and honor the survivors who continue to carry those memories forward.

Printed in Great Britain
by Amazon